A PROBLEM SHARED

TALKING ABOUT
MENTAL HEALTH

Louise Spilsbury

PowerKiDS
press™

New York

Published in 2023 by The Rosen Publishing Group, Inc.
29 East 21st Street, New York, NY 10010

Editor: Amy Pimperton

Designer and illustrator: Collaborate

Cataloging-in-Publication Data

Names: Spilsbury, Louise.
Title: Talking about mental health / Louise Spilsbury.
Description: New York : Powerkids Press, 2023. | Series: A problem shared | Includes glossary and index.
Identifiers: ISBN 9781725338814 (pbk.) | ISBN 9781725338838 (library bound) | ISBN 9781725338821 (6pack) | ISBN 9781725338845 (ebook)
Subjects: LCSH: Mental health--Juvenile literature. | Mental illness--Juvenile literature.
Classification: LCC RA790.53 S645 2023 | DDC 362.196'89--dc23

Manufactured in the United States of America

CPSIA Compliance Information: Batch #CSPK23. For further information contact Rosen Publishing, New York, New York at 1-800-237-9932.

Find us on

CONTENTS

WHAT ARE MENTAL HEALTH PROBLEMS?

Mental health, like physical health, is something that affects us all. When people go through a time of mental health problems, it affects their mood, thinking, and behavior. Someone might feel so low, worried, stressed, or confused that it becomes difficult, or even impossible, for them to cope.

Mental health problems are really common and can happen to anyone at some time in their life. Mental health problems include:

- depression – a feeling of low mood that lasts for a long time
- anxiety – feeling worried, tense, or afraid – particularly about things that are about to happen, or which we think could happen in the future
- eating problems – when difficult and painful feelings cause people to eat too little or too much food.

SHARING PROBLEMS

Having a mental health problem can be upsetting, confusing, and frightening. It can make people feel very lonely and scared. Even though everyone's experience of mental health will be unique, talking about the problem will help.

Have you heard the saying "A problem shared is a problem halved"? Sharing problems relieves some of the anxiety and gives other people the chance to help you. In this book we meet some people who have shared mental health problems and find out what happened when they did.

ASK FOR HELP

Emotional well-being, or mental health, is just as important as physical health. Someone with a broken arm would ask for help and it's the same with mental health. If you have a problem and something is worrying you, it's vital that you get the help you need.

STRESSED BY SCHOOL

At times everyone feels a bit stressed by the pressure to do well at school. But what if this stress becomes so hard to cope with that everyday life becomes impossible? This is Tomasz's story.

Until a few months ago, I was top of my class for almost every subject. But recently I've fallen way behind. The work feels harder and I've lost all my confidence. I do try to concentrate, but sometimes the stress builds up. I feel I'm in a dark fog and I can't think or see straight.

I just don't feel like I'm good enough any more. I feel nervous going to school and I'm sad all the time and feel detached from everything. Sometimes I feel physically sick or I get such a bad headache that I have to miss school – and that makes me worry that I'll get even further behind!

Tomasz

WHAT SHOULD TOMASZ DO?

1 Work harder? If he makes an effort, his grades will go up and he can stop worrying.

2 Cheer up and try to forget about his problems so they go away?

3 Talk to a parent or teacher about his anxiety and get help?

RED FLAG

If you feel so worried or anxious about something that it makes you feel physically ill in some way, that's a clear red flag that something is wrong and you need to do something about it.

EXPLORING SOLUTIONS

Tomasz realizes things are getting worse and he finally works up the courage to talk to a teacher who he likes. This is what happened.

Mr. Masters

When Tomasz told me about his worries, we explored ways to help to reduce the stress he is feeling. We talked about Tomasz setting himself smaller, more achievable targets, instead of worrying about getting the highest grades. This should help him to feel more in control and less disappointed.

He is also going to take regular 10-minute breaks when he is doing homework. It can be difficult to do this when you're stressed about getting things done, but it can help you to concentrate better.

Tomasz will ask his older brother for help with harder subjects and will ask me for extra help if he is still confused. Talking to his parents about how he feels will also help. He's going to see the school counselor regularly, so he has someone else to talk to about his anxiety and who can also suggest ways to help him keep calm.

Concentrating on one task for a long time is tiring for your eyes and brain. Taking a break for 10 minutes for every 30 minutes of homework you do can make a huge difference to how you feel.

TOP TIPS

Doing regular exercise can clear the mind and help you to relax. This reduces stress and tension and makes you feel less anxious. It doesn't matter what type of exercise you do – cycling, hockey, martial arts, tennis, football, basketball, and swimming are all great, but make sure you choose a sport you enjoy.

I DON'T HAVE A PROBLEM

Between the ages of 8 to 14, the human body goes through the big changes we call puberty. These changes can cause some people to feel insecure about the way they look and make them feel out of control or anxious. This is Grace's story.

Grace

I've been on a diet for a while as I really need to lose weight and I totally hate the way I look. I skip breakfast and tell Mom I'll get something on the way to school. I pretend to eat the lunches she makes, but I throw them in the bin instead.

I'm just trying to be healthy and get slim, but Kat – who was my best friend until last week – seems to think I have a problem. I don't! I feel so much better when I'm controlling what I eat. I'm so angry because Kat told my mom I've been hiding food and not eating and that she thinks I need help. I think she's just jealous that I'm losing weight!

RED FLAG

Eating too little or too much food can be a red flag for mental health problems. An eating disorder isn't about gaining or losing weight. It's a mental health condition where someone thinks they're not good enough and want to change. Problems with food usually mean someone needs help working through other problems.

WHAT DO YOU THINK?

Do you think Kat did the right thing by telling Grace's mom? What would you have done? What might have happened if Kat did nothing?

TRYING TO HELP

Kat didn't want to lose Grace's friendship, but she was so worried about Grace she knew she had to do something. She knew that telling Grace's mom was the right thing to do. This is Kat's side of the story.

Kat

I was really upset when Grace was mad at me for telling her mom. But I was so scared she was making herself ill. She was getting so thin, but she wore baggy clothes so her mom wouldn't notice, and she pretended to her mom she was eating.

It wasn't just the food thing. She seemed unhappy and all she talked about was how she was going to look so much better when she lost more weight.

Things are so much better now that Grace is getting help. She sees an eating disorder nurse and has been talking about her feelings. She looks healthier and seems a bit more like her old self. She was mad at me for a while, but we talked about it and made up. People have been telling her she is lucky to have a friend like me who wanted to help her and now we're closer than ever.

TOP TIPS

These are some helpful ways to take care of your body and mind:

- eat a healthy balanced diet to help your brain and body develop properly
- do regular exercise to maintain a healthy weight
- focus on the things you like about yourself and the parts of your body that you like, not the things you don't
- think about what advice you would give a friend if they were having negative thoughts about the way they look and use that advice yourself.

I LIVE IN FEAR

We all get anxious and worried sometimes. It's natural. But when fear and anxiety stop you living your life, then it becomes a problem. This is Hamed's story.

Omar, my stepdad, was driving me home from school one day a couple of months ago. A car driving in the opposite direction was overtaking and was heading straight for us.

The other driver swerved at the last minute and crashed into a tree. We were OK because the other car only clipped ours, but the other driver was badly hurt.

Now I can't sleep. I have horrible dreams about the crash and the nightmares feel so real that I feel panicky and scared even when I am awake. I hate going in cars now and I try to avoid anything that reminds me of the accident – like being near roads and even walking on the pavement. It's stopping me going out with friends and even makes it hard for me to get to school.

Hamed

RED FLAG

Finding it hard to fall asleep at night or waking in the early hours can be a sure sign that something is wrong. Lack of sleep makes the brain a bit foggy and that makes it even harder for people to cope with things that are upsetting them. The only way to deal with the concerns that are keeping you awake is to talk about and deal with them.

FINDING CALMNESS

Hamed's stepdad, Omar, takes him to the doctor, who recommends that Hamed sees a therapist. She can help him talk through his fears and explore ways of coping with them.

I often went with Hamed when he talked to the therapist. At first I wasn't sure how it could help, but after a few weeks I can see how talking to her has made a real difference to Hamed. She's been building up Hamed's confidence and has even helped him walk on a pavement next to a busy road, talking him though his fears while we walked.

Omar

We've been following her suggestions and walking on quieter roads to school and going for short drives very early on a Sunday morning when there are few cars about. Hamed is still scared about getting in the car, but while we drive we both practice the deep breathing and other relaxation techniques the therapist taught him to help him feel calmer. It will take a while for him to feel safe again, but he is making progress and I'm so proud of him and so grateful to his therapist.

TOP TIPS

Shoulder-roll breathing is a technique you can practice to help you feel calmer when you're stressed:

- get into a comfortable sitting position
- as you slowly breathe in through your nose, lift your shoulders up to your ears
- as you slowly breathe out, lower your shoulders back down.

Do this at least five times and concentrate completely on what you're doing.

This should help you to feel calmer.

WORN DOWN BY WORRY

When families have problems with money, it's not only parents who get stressed. Around a quarter of young people say they've been worried about their family struggling to pay the bills at some point. This is Harriet's story.

Harriet

We've never had a lot of money, but things have got a lot worse since Mom lost her job. Dad works part-time, so now they have to borrow money to pay the bills. They don't talk to me about it, but I hear them arguing about money all the time. I'm scared we might lose our house.

I feel guilty about taking lunch money, so I try not to eat too much and I try and be as cheerful as I can because I'm also worried that if Mum and Dad get even unhappier they might end up getting a divorce.

Sometimes the worries swirl around in my head and I start to panic. My throat feels like its closing up and it gets hard to breathe. My heart races and I feel shaky and sweaty. Sometimes I worry that I'm really ill.

If you feel so anxious that you can't breathe, you may be having a panic attack. It does not mean that you are ill, but it is serious and a red flag that you should get help.

WHAT SHOULD HARRIET DO?

1 Stop worrying about money? It's up to the adults to sort out money worries.

2 Try to find ways to save money, like making a packed lunch?

3 Talk to someone: her parents or a school counselor, for example?

Which option do you think will make the biggest difference?

SHARING CONCERNS

After a bad panic attack, Harriet gets so scared there might be something seriously wrong with her that she talks to her mom. This is what happened next.

Harriet's mom

I felt terrible when Harriet told me that she'd heard us argue about money and that she'd been having panic attacks. I gave her a big hug and told her that I'm looking for a new job and whatever happens, her dad and I will be there to love and support her. We're arguing because we're stressed, but we do still love each other.

The panic attacks have really scared her because they make her feel like her body is out of control. I told her that panic attacks are her body reacting to all the anxiety, so next time Harriet starts to feel overwhelmed, she's promised to tell me about it so we can deal with it together.

We're going to set aside time to do some things together that will help us all to feel more relaxed, too, such as watching a movie or taking the dog for a walk.

SIDE-BY-SIDE

Harriet found that walking side-by-side with her mom made talking about their problems much easier than if they were talking face-to-face.

TOP TIPS

If you often feel weighed down by worries, set aside 10 minutes a day to do something to help stop anxious thoughts from taking over.

For example, you could write down what's worrying you and some things you could do to lessen those worries. Then, put your notes in a box and try to forget them for the rest of the day.

DEALING WITH PAIN

People may try a variety of different ways to cope with depression and mental health problems. Sometimes they may even hurt or harm themselves to escape the emotional pain they feel. This is Riley's story.

I began to feel depressed after years of being bullied at school. First it was just teasing but now it's really nasty. I've had anonymous texts during the night saying no one likes me and that I should just leave and make everyone's lives better. It's a nightmare and I feel like I'm screaming inside.

The only thing that makes me feel better is scratching my arms, and pinching myself so hard that I bruise the skin. The pain makes me forget the bullying. It makes me feel stronger and like I'm in control of something in my life.

The problem is that the sense of relief lasts only a few minutes and then I feel worse because I feel ashamed. Feeling ashamed just makes me feel lonelier than ever and that makes me hurt myself again.

People who self-harm often go to great lengths to cover it up, so if someone you know is behaving a little differently and starts wearing wide wristbands and bracelets or long sleeves and pants even when it is hot, it might be a red flag that they are self-harming.

TOP TIPS

Telling someone is vital if you're going to stop something like self-harming, but it can be really hard to talk to others about it, so take it step-by-step:

- decide who you're going to tell
- choose when and where to tell them
- practice saying it out loud
- imagine their response.

23

THE BLAME GAME

Riley decides to tell her mom and tries to pick a time to talk when her mom isn't too tired or busy and when no one else is in the house. But things still don't quite go to plan ...

Riley's mom

Riley has been very difficult recently. She's been holed up in her room most evenings and doesn't say much when she does come downstairs. I felt upset and angry when she told me what she'd been doing up there. How could she be hurting herself on purpose, scratching, bruising, and pinching her lovely skin?

I told her it was a very childish and silly thing to do and that people will think she's just attention seeking. I imagine she got the idea off social media. I'm so disappointed in her. I don't think I can trust her, so I've told her to keep her bedroom door open from now on. I don't want to upset her, but I'm going to have to watch her like a hawk to make sure she doesn't do this self-harming thing again.

WHAT SHOULD RILEY DO?

1 Make more of an effort to stop self-harming?

2 Make more of an effort to ignore the bullying

3 Talk to another adult or see her doctor?

Which of these different choices are likely to help the most?

TALK ABOUT IT

If someone you speak to doesn't understand how you feel, don't give up. Try speaking to another family member, a trusted adult, or a doctor.

A NEW UNDERSTANDING

Riley has scratched herself so hard in one place that it became infected, so her mom takes her to the doctor to get it checked. The doctor realizes she needs to treat more than Riley's sore arm.

Dr. Khan

When someone comes in with a pattern of bruises or cuts, it is easy to see they have been self-harming. People usually self-harm because something is upsetting them, such as being bullied at school. Self-harming can cause long-term damage and sadly it can become a habit that is hard to stop. Sometimes people feel that it's the only way they can cope, but there are other, much healthier ways.

The first thing to do is deal with the trigger for, or cause of, self-harming, for example by informing a school if bullying is the issue. To stop the self-harming habit, people can try other ways of letting their emotions out. They could try holding an ice cube in their hand until it melts or writing down their negative feelings and then ripping the paper up and throwing it away.

WHAT HAPPENED NEXT ?

Riley's mum realized that she had been too hard on Riley and hadn't tried to understand what the real problem was. She hadn't been able to see beyond her own anger at Riley.

Together, Riley and her mum made a plan to talk to the school to stop the bullying. Now that Riley feels her mum understands, she doesn't feel so alone and feels much more positive about the future.

TOP TIPS

You can see a doctor on your own, but it's usually helpful to have a parent, guardian, or other trusted adult with you, or to sit in the waiting room so you know someone is there if you need them.

MENTAL HEALTH MATTERS!

Having a mental health problem can be very lonely and every day can feel like a battle. But help is available and things can and will get better if you share how you're feeling.

We all get overwhelmed sometimes. One thing we can all do is to talk honestly and openly on a regular basis about things that worry us. Simply speaking our fears out loud can make them feel smaller.

Talking about our feelings can help us to stay in good mental health and help us to deal with more difficult times when they do come along.

You might feel better after talking to family or friends who offer practical ideas or help – or simply give you a comforting hug or a shoulder to cry on.

Doctors can put you in touch with local mental health services that can help. Or you can call a helpline, such as one of those listed on page 32 of this book. The most important thing to do is to keep trying and talking until you find the person who can help to make that change.

As well as finding help, take time to help yourself in other ways. For example:

- help to care for others, for example you could volunteer for a local charity. This makes us feel needed and valued, which boosts our self-esteem.

- do things you love and can lose yourself in. Enjoying yourself can help beat stress. Doing an activity you enjoy and are good at it means you achieve something, which boosts your self-esteem too.

GLOSSARY

anonymous when a person isn't named so their identity remains a secret

ashamed feeling embarrassed or guilty about something

counselor someone who is trained to give advice on personal problems, such as a psychologist or therapist

detached in this instance, feeling like you are not connected to what is happening around you

habit something you do regularly, usually without thinking about it

negative feelings about something that are not positive, good or happy

puberty the time when a child's body changes to an adult's body

self-esteem how you feel about yourself; your confidence

self-harm to hurt yourself on purpose

therapist a person trained to treat people who have mental health illnesses

trigger an event or feeling that causes something to happen

unique one of a kind

vital necessary